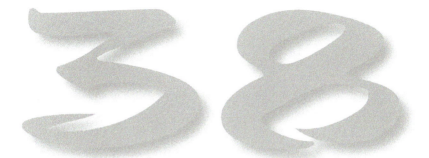

Thirty-Eight
LATIN STORIES

Teacher's Guide

Composed By
ANNE H. GROTON AND JAMES M. MAY

Bolchazy-Carducci Publishers, Inc.
Mundelein, Illinois USA

General Editor: Laurie Haight Keenan
Contributing Editor: James Chochola
Cover Design & Typography: Adam Phillip Velez

Thirty-eight Latin Stories
Teacher's Guide

Anne H. Groton and James M. May

© 2004 Bolchazy-Carducci Publishers, Inc.

Bolchazy-Carducci Publishers, Inc.
1570 Baskin Road
Mundelein, Illinois 60060
www.bolchazy.com

Printed in the United States of America
2011
by CreateSpace

ISBN 978-0-86516-591-5

TABLE OF CONTENTS

PREFACE TO THE TEACHER'S GUIDE

In response to frequent requests for some help in translating the selections in *Thirty-Eight Latin Stories*, we have created this guide for teachers, homeschoolers, and people who are learning Latin on their own. All of our English translations are intended as straightforward keys to the stories; they do not claim to be artistic or literary masterpieces. We have aimed for consistency, wherever possible, in our choice of vocabulary and syntax. When a literal rendering of a Latin idiom would have resulted in awkward or stilted English, we have opted for a more natural-sounding, colloquial translation, but in those cases we have included a word-for-word translation (*lit.* = "literal") in square brackets. Also in square brackets are any English words that must be supplied to complete the sense at points where the Latin text is elliptical.

We hope that the Teacher's Guide will be of service to those who are using *Thirty-Eight Latin Stories* to teach themselves, their children, or their students the basics of Latin.

Anne H. Groton and James M. May
July 2004

Translation of story for Chapters 1–3:
PANDORA'S BOX

Iapetus has two sons, Prometheus and Epimetheus. Prometheus is a man of great wisdom; Epimetheus is a man without wisdom. Jupiter gives a beautiful woman, Pandora, to Epimetheus. Prometheus often warns Epimetheus about Pandora: "Epimetheus, you are making a mistake! You do not see the danger. You ought not to accept the woman." Epimetheus loves Pandora; he does not think about the danger. Jupiter gives a box to Epimetheus; it is not permitted to open the box. But Pandora is curious: "What is in the box? Much money? A great number of jewels?" The woman opens the box. Many forms of evil fly out and go wandering around! But Pandora preserves hope in the box. Even if life is full of misfortunes, we always have hope.

Translation of story for Chapter 4:
THE TRAGIC STORY OF PHAËTHON

Phaëthon is the son of Phoebus. Phaëthon's friend is doubtful about the report of [Phaëthon's] divine origin: "You are not the son of a god. You do not have the gifts of the gods. Your story is not true." Great anger moves Phaëthon: "I *am* the son of a god! Phoebus, give [me] proof!" Phaëthon calls. Phoebus hears the boy and without delay flies down from heaven. "My son, what do you desire?" Phoebus asks. "Money? Wisdom? A life without cares?" Phaëthon answers, "I desire to hold the reins and to drive the chariot of the sun." O foolish boy! Your plan is bad. You ought not to desire the duties of the gods. Phoebus warns his son, but the boy does not see the great dangers. The horses are strong; Phaëthon is not strong. Without its true master, the chariot goes astray in the sky. What do we see? Down from the sky falls Phaëthon. O wicked fortune!

Translation of story for Chapter 5:
THE ADVENTURES OF IO

Jupiter, king of the gods, was in love with beautiful Io, but he feared the anger of Juno. He therefore changed the shape of Io: "Juno will see not a woman but a cow," Jupiter thought. Juno was not stupid: "Do you have a gift, my husband? Will you give [this] beautiful cow to Juno? Give [her to me], if you love me!" Jupiter therefore gave the cow to Juno. There remained with the cow a huge watchman, Argus. Argus had a hundred eyes. Mercury overcame Argus, but Io was not yet free: an evil gadfly remained with the cow. Io wandered through the lands; she saw many nations, but she did not have her own true form. Poor woman! Will you always have the shape of a cow? Is your punishment not enough?

Juno's anger was not perpetual: Jupiter gave human form [back] to Io; then Io gave birth to a son. You will see the hundred eyes of Argus in the tail of the peacock.

Translation of story for Chapter 6:
THE CURSE OF ATREUS

The sons of Pelops were Atreus and Thyestes. Thyestes seduces the wife of Atreus; then Atreus discovers the crime and is unable to bear [it]. Therefore he plots treachery against his brother: "I am full of rage! Because of this I will kill and cut up my brother's small sons. Then I will cook their limbs and offer a dinner to Thyestes." He kills the boys; Thyestes sees his own sons dead on the table. O wretched Thyestes! Now you have nothing. But, Atreus, because of your great crimes your sons will pay great penalties. In the souls of your sons your ancient guilt will remain; it will be eternal. What ought we to think about your treachery, O Atreus? You were not able to overcome your anger; therefore your reputation will always be evil. Few good people will praise you and [the way you conducted] your life, but many [good] people will blame [you and it].

Translation of story for Chapter 7:
CLEOBIS AND BITON

Cleobis and Biton were the sons of Cydippe. Cydippe was a priestess of the goddess Juno. Cydippe desired to see the great statue of Juno. But the statue was far away, and Cydippe was not able to walk; the boys did not possess oxen. Cleobis and Biton loved Cydippe; they therefore pulled the wagon themselves. The work was hard, but Cydippe's sons were hardy. Now Cydippe was able to see the statue; because of this she prayed to Juno: "O beautiful goddess! Cleobis and Biton have good character and valor. Therefore give my sons the best reward." On account of the prayers of Cydippe Juno immediately [*lit.* without delay] gave the boys death without pain. Cleobis and Biton are now happy in eternal peace.

Translation of story for Chapter 8:
LAOCOÖN AND THE TROJAN HORSE

The Greeks were waging war against [*lit.* with] the Trojans. At night they leave a large wooden horse beneath the gates of the city of Troy [*lit.* city Troy]. The Trojans find the horse there. "The Greeks are dedicating the horse to Minerva," they say. "If we take [*lit.* will take] the Greeks' gift to the temple of the goddess, we will have peace and lead a life of good fortune." But Laocoön, a priest of great virtue and wisdom, dares to warn the people: "You are thinking irrationally [*lit.* without reason], O Trojans. If there are troops inside the horse, we will be in great danger. You ought never to trust the Greeks, for Greeks are always deceitful." Then he strikes the horse with a spear. Minerva's anger is great; the goddess sends two serpents out of the sea. O poor Laocoön! The wicked snakes strangle you and your two sons! The Trojans fear the goddess; they pull the horse into the city. Laocoön's reasoning teaches the Trojans nothing.

Translation of story for Chapter 9:
NISUS AND EURYALUS

Aeneas was leading the Trojans against the Rutulians. While it was night and the troops were asleep, the leaders of the Trojans were holding a meeting in the camp. Nisus and Euryalus, Trojan youths, dare to come to them. "O great men," says Nisus, "if you send [*lit.* will send] me along with Euryalus to the camp of the Rutulians, not only will we slay many people, but we will also snatch much loot from them; for sleep holds them." "I praise the courage and manliness of these young men!" exclaims Iulus, son of that [famed] Aeneas. "Farewell!"

Now Nisus and Euryalus come into the camp of the Rutulians. They kill one, then many others. Euryalus steals the uniform of one, the helmet of another. With this loot they flee. But Volcens, a leader of the Rutulians, sees those Trojans and summons other Rutulians. The glint of that helmet leads them to Euryalus. Nisus sees him in danger and dares to save his friend. He kills Volcens, but that man first [*lit.* earlier] kills Euryalus. Then others overcome Nisus; he falls [dead] upon the body of Euryalus.

Vergil will write this whole story and give eternal fame to these Trojans.

Translation of story for Chapter 10:
AURORA AND TITHONUS

The goddess Aurora was in love with Tithonus, a handsome man. She therefore comes to Jupiter: "O king of the gods, " she says, "hear me! My Tithonus is not a god; after a few years he will reach old age. If you grant [*lit.* will grant] him eternal life, I will always praise you." Foolish Aurora! You do not see the great danger of that gift. Jupiter gives immortality to Tithonus, but he [Tithonus], while he remains alive, grows old. Time slips away: now Aurora is pretty, Tithonus is not. His body, wrinkled and bent, is no longer strong; wisdom does not remain in his mind. What will Aurora do? Will she be able to restore beauty to Tithonus? She ponders and seizes a plan: "O Tithonus, my love! I will turn you into a cricket; then you will be able to chirp without blame. You will live in this cage, and I will love you always."

Translation of story for Chapter 11:

ULYSSES AND THE CYCLOPS

After the Trojan War Ulysses comes with twelve men to the land of the Cyclopes. In a cave they find cheese of good quality. While they are eating it, the Cyclops Polyphemus leads huge sheep into the same cave and sees the Greeks: "What are you doing in my cave? You will pay penalties if you have evil plans in mind." "We are sailing from Troy," Ulysses says to him. "What will you give to us?" But Polyphemus exclaims, "Fool! What will you, you and your dear men, give to me?" Without delay he seizes and eats a few men! Then he asks, "What is your name?" Ulysses answers, "Nobody." While sleep overcomes Polyphemus, the Greeks make a plot. They sharpen a log in the flame and thrust it into the eye of the Cyclops [*lit.* that one]. O poor Polyphemus! Things are not going well for you. Other Cyclopes come, but they do not perceive the real danger. "Nobody is killing me!" calls Polyphemus. "Fine!" they say. "Goodbye!" The Greeks therefore are able to escape from the cave. The blinded Cyclops hears these words: "Farewell! I am not Nobody, but Ulysses!"

Translation of story for Chapter 12:

A GIFT BEARING GREEKS

In Asia Minor there was a great city, Troy. King Priam lived there. His son Paris had stolen Helen, a beautiful Greek woman. Because of this crime many Greeks had come to Asia and for a long time had waged a bitter war against [*lit.* with] the Trojans. They had not, however, been able to conquer the walls of the city. But then Epeus, one of the Greeks, offered them this plan: "If we make [*lit.* will make] a great wooden horse and give [*lit.* will give] it to the Trojans, we will be able to conquer them; for we will have hidden Greeks inside the horse."

"You have instructed us well," said the Greeks, and without delay they carried out that treacherous plot. After the war Aeneas, a Trojan leader, said, "We did not see the troops in the horse; we led it into the city. Therefore the Greeks were able to conquer us. The gods had perceived our bad fortune in advance and had fled from our city."

Translation of story for Chapter 13:
ECHO AND HANDSOME NARCISSUS

Narcissus was a handsome boy. Many girls loved him; he loved none of them. He loved himself alone and spent his life in the woods. The nymph Echo had loved Narcissus for a long time, but she had never been able to express her love to him: she was able to repeat only the last word of another [person]. If Narcissus called, "Are you here?" Echo called, "Here!" If he said, "Where are you? Come!" she said, "Come!" But Narcissus did not come to her, and Echo therefore did not live long. She lost her entire body; her voice, however, we hear even now.

Meanwhile Narcissus saw his reflection in a pool and was not able to move his eyes away. He was conquered by [his] great love [of] himself. Time passed; Narcissus remained in the same spot. His friends were not able to find him. In front of that very pool where he had been, there was now a beautiful flower. Its name will forever be Narcissus.

People ought not to love themselves too much.

Translation of story for Chapter 14:
EUROPA AND THE BULL

Jupiter, king of the gods, saw Europa, the daughter of Agenor. Overcome with love for her [lit. of her], he said, "I will not be able to live without this beautiful woman. But what should I do? This maiden, if I overcome [lit. will overcome] her by force, will not love me, and my wife Juno, if she discovers [lit. will discover] my treachery, will chastise me. By craftiness, therefore, I ought to lead Europa to me."

Jupiter gave himself the form of a bull. Swiftly he raced from his citadel in the sky through the clouds to the earth. Europa together with her friends had wandered into remote regions. That great bull came to them. The other girls fled; Europa alone (for she had always loved animals) remained with the bull. Europa held his neck in her arms; immediately [lit. without delay] he dragged her across the sea!

Europa sensed danger and cried out, "O!" Jupiter said, "Beautiful woman, no evil thoughts are in my mind. I am not a bull, but a god. Not death, but fame and glory will come to you, for great poets will link your name with mine."

Translation of story for Chapter 15:

HOW THE AEGEAN GOT ITS NAME

Theseus and his father, King Aegeus, lived in Athens. At that time the citizens were paying penalties to the king of the island Crete: they were sending seven boys and the same number of girls to him. These fourteen victims were offering their lives to the Minotaur. To his father Theseus said, "I am not able to bear this terrible custom! I myself am not afraid of the Minotaur. I will find him, and, if I am able [*lit.* will be able], I will defeat him with my strength. I entrust my fortune to the gods. You will see white sails, my father, if I escape [*lit.* will escape] death." And so Theseus joined [*lit.* joined himself with] the other victims and sailed across the sea to Crete. There by his own labor he was able to conquer the Minotaur and, by the artfulness of his lover Ariadne, to escape.

For a long time Aegeus had been waiting on a cliff for his son; now he was able to see his son's very ship. But the sails are black, not white! Foolish Theseus had not retained his own plan in his memory; he had not changed the sails. Wretched Aegeus threw himself without delay into the "Aegean" Sea.

Translation of story for Chapter 16:

THE WRATH OF ACHILLES

Achilles was not only a brave and strong hero, but also the son of the goddess Thetis. [Together] with Agamemnon and other Greeks, he [*lit.* that one] had come to Troy and had waged a long and difficult war. But now after nine years bitter wrath moved him; for Agamemnon had taken for himself a captive woman dear to him [= Achilles]. And so Achilles called his mother: "Help me!" In the sea Thetis heard him and raced to him: "I understand your feelings, my sweet son," she said. "All the Greeks ought to hold you in great honor; for without you they are not able to conquer the Trojans. Consider these things: if you flee [*lit.* will flee] now from this war, you will have little glory, but a long life; if, however, you remain [*lit.* will remain] in this place, you will find great glory, but you will lose your life."

"O blessed mother, be of good cheer!" said Achilles. "For all human beings life is brief. I myself do not fear swift death. I will remain here, but since huge anger grips me, I will not wage war." How great is the power of anger!

Translation of story for Chapter 17:
THE MYRMIDONS (ANT PEOPLE)

Once upon a time Aeacus was ruling Aegina, which had taken its name from the name of the mother of Aeacus, with whom Jupiter had united [*lit.* united himself] in love. Juno, who had never been able to tolerate the bad habits of Jupiter, perceived this deed and held it in [her] memory. After many years she sent death to all who were living on the island of Aegina [*lit.* island Aegina]. "O father Jupiter," Aeacus called, "Juno has annihilated my entire nation! Help me, your son, whom you love and whom you ought not to neglect." The god heard him and without delay began to change the ants into human beings! And so Jupiter, for whom nothing is too difficult, created men and women out of small animals. (Do I speak the truth, or not?)

The son of Aeacus was Peleus, whose son was that [celebrated] Achilles, leader of the Myrmidons.

Translation of story for Chapter 18:
A WEDDING INVITATION

Greetings, O gods and goddesses! Our friend Peleus has great plans: he will marry [*lit.* lead into matrimony] the nymph Thetis. Therefore you are being invited by me, Jupiter, to Thessaly. Expect excellent games and delightful feasts. You ought, however, to be warned about these dangers: 1. Since Peleus is a mortal, his mind will be terrified if we seem [*lit.* will seem] too powerful; 2. Whoever dares to come without a gift will be punished by me. Choose types of gifts that will be praised by all who see [*lit.* will see] them.

You alone, O goddess Discord, are not being invited, for you are loved by no one. If you come [*lit.* will come], every god on Mount Olympus will be moved with rage. Among friends discord ought not to be tolerated.

Penalties will be paid by whichever god [*lit.* that god who] neglects [*lit.* will neglect] his duty. Farewell!

Translation of story for Chapter 19:
THE JUDGMENT OF PARIS

The goddess Discord, who alone had not been invited to the wedding of Peleus and Thetis, was moved by anger. She therefore threw into the palace of the immortal gods a golden apple, on which had been inscribed these letters: "For the fairest." To whom should the apple be given? To Juno or to Venus or to Minerva? Even Jupiter himself is afraid to make a judgment! And so those three goddesses come to Paris, the son of the Trojan king.

"O dear young man," they say, "which of us, in your opinion, is the fairest? A great gift will be provided for you by the goddess whom you choose [*lit.* will choose]." Whom will Paris choose? By which gift will the mind of the judge be moved? Juno is able to make him a king, Minerva, a general. Venus, however, is able to give him Helen, the fairest of all [mortal] women.

Paris was conquered by love and gave the golden apple to Venus. And so (if the report of these events is accurate) Helen was kidnapped and led to a new location, Troy. Which war was waged on account of that woman?

Translation of story for Chapter 20:
THE LABORS OF HERCULES

Who has not heard the name of Hercules? I will now say a few [words] about his mighty deeds.

Fortune had led Hercules, a Greek hero whose strength was extraordinary, into slavery. Eurystheus had assigned to that poor man twelve onerous labors. But Hercules had not been conquered by fear; he could be terrified neither by strange animals nor by human beings of the sort that is never free from crimes. With [his] hands alone, Hercules conquered a huge lion; he captured a swift deer, whose horns were golden, and brought her to Mycenae from the place in which he had found her. Then he was sent by Eurystheus against Cerberus, a fierce dog; even this beast he was able to remove from the very gate of Pluto!

After these and other deeds Hercules was freed from his labors. But what reward was given to him? None. What was the fruit of his labors? Glory and perpetual remembrance in the verses of the poets.

Translation of story for Chapter 21:
THE GOLDEN AGE RETURNS

Now a great and new age begins. A boy is being born, and a golden race is coming. The world will be freed from its deep dread. That boy will receive the life of the gods and will see the gods, and he himself will be seen by them. He will rule the world with ancient virtues. As soon as he is [*lit.* will be] able to read [about] the merits and accomplishments of his parent and to understand excellence, the happy fields will provide sweet fruits for all people. There will remain, however, a few vices that will compel men to try out the sea with ships, that will compel men to gird cities with walls. There will even be other wars, and mighty Achilles will again be sent to Troy. When maturity has [*lit.* will have] made this boy a man, however, the seas will be abandoned by the travelers, and the sailors will not exchange goods for the sake of money. The hardy farmer will free his bulls from the yoke; the soil will not be touched by the hoes; the entire earth will produce all things.

Translation of story for Chapter 22:
CICERO REPORTS HIS VICTORY OVER CATILINE

On this day, citizens, by means of my labors, counsels, and risks, I have rescued the republic, the lives, goods, fortunes of all of you, the senate-house and this beautiful city, from fire and sword. Now, citizens, since you already hold captive the wicked leaders of a wicked war, you ought to reflect on your good hope [for the future]. Catiline has been driven out of the heart of the city. He was the one who was feared by all, so long as he was contained within the city walls. Now that man, so fierce, so bold, so vigilant in crime, so diligent in evil-doings, has been removed. Although all of these [*lit.* all these] developments, citizens, have been managed by me, they nevertheless seem to have been both administered and provided for at the command and with the counsel of the immortal gods. For on many occasions the immortal gods have nourished the hope and trust of this republic. But at this time you ought to give most glorious thanks to them. For you have been delivered from a most cruel and miserable death, delivered without slaughter, without bloodshed, without [recourse to] an army.

In your memory, citizens, our accomplishments will be cherished; the praise, fame, and glory [deriving from our accomplishments] will be vigorous; they will live on in literature and endure. We can be at peace forever, citizens.

Translation of story for Chapter 23:
WATCHING THE ORATOR AT WORK

Now the great orator rises, ready to plead his case: every spot on the benches is occupied; the platform is full [of people]; the jurors, wishing to hear his every word, call for silence. The eyes of all are directed toward him. Then there are many expressions of admiration, many shouts of praise. The orator touches the emotions of his listeners. When he wishes them to be moved by fear or pity, they are terrified, overcome by fear, or they weep, overcome by pity.

Often you will be able to make a judgment about an orator even if you will have caught sight of him not while you are sitting close to him and listening attentively, but with a mere glance while you are passing by. You will see a juror yawning, talking with someone else, sometimes even wandering about, sending [someone] to find out the time, ignoring the words spoken by the orator. This case lacks a true orator, one who is able to move the jurors' emotions with his speech. If, however, you see [lit. will have seen] alert jurors who appear [lit. will appear] to be in the act of receiving instruction about something or who are caught and are held [lit. will be held] suspended, like birds [attracted] by some birdcall, you will recognize the signs of a true orator and of one performing oratorical work well.

Translation of story for Chapter 24:

CAESAR'S CAMP IS ATTACKED BY BELGIANS

When the cavalry had been sent out ahead, Caesar was leading six legions; behind them he had stationed the baggage train for the whole army; our horsemen, when the river had been crossed, engaged in battle with the enemy's cavalry. Those [horsemen] were repeatedly retreating into the woods to their own [men] and [then] again, from the woods, making an attack against our [men]. Our soldiers dared to pursue them only up to the edge of the woods. Meanwhile the six legions, as soon as [*lit.* when first] they arrived, after their weapons had been put aside, began to fortify the camp. When the first baggage carts of our army were noticed by those who were lurking in the woods, they rushed forth at full strength and made an attack against our cavalrymen. After [our] cavalrymen had easily been driven back, they raced with incredible speed to the river. And so the enemy seemed at one [single] time to be near the woods and in the river and close at hand [*lit.* in our hands]. With the same speed they ran toward our camp and [toward] those who were engaged [*lit.* had been occupied] in work.

Everything had to be done by Caesar all at once [*lit.* at one time]: the standard had to be planted, the signal that ordered them to take up arms had to be given by the trumpet; the soldiers had to be recalled from their labor; the line of battle had to be prepared. The shortness of the time and the arrival of the enemy impeded the majority [*lit.* a large part] of these activities. And so, on account of the proximity and speed of the enemy, the generals were not waiting around for Caesar's command but were doing by themselves the things that seemed best [to them to do].

Translation of story for Chapter 25:

THE CHARACTER OF CATILINE'S FOLLOWERS

But why are we talking so long about one enemy, and about an enemy who already declares that he is an enemy, and whom, because a wall lies between [us], I do not fear? Are we saying nothing about these [conspirators] who are in the middle of the city, who are [right here] with us? For I will describe to you, citizens, the types of men that furnish those troops [*lit.* out of which those troops are furnished]. One type consists of [*lit.* is of] those who, [though] in great debt, still have great possessions, induced by the love of which, they can in no way be freed from debt. But I do not think that these men should be feared, because they can be dissuaded from their opinion.

The other type consists of [*lit.* is of] those who, [although] they are oppressed by debt, nevertheless are expecting the power and public offices that they think they are able to acquire when the government has been thrown into confusion. They should not hope for this! For they [*lit.* those people] must realize this: that, first of all, I myself am vigilant, am present to help, am looking out for the republic; next, that there is great courage among the good men, great harmony of the social orders, a very large multitude, large troops of soldiers; finally, that against so great a force of evil the immortal gods will give aid to this unconquered people, to this renowned dominion, to this beautiful city. They do not hope, do they, that in the ashes of the city and in the blood of its citizens, they will [have the chance to] be either consuls or dictators or even kings?

Translation of story for Chapter 26:
THE VIRTUES OF THE ORATOR CATO

Indeed, who of our contemporary orators reads Cato? Or who is familiar with him? But, good gods, what a man! I omit [his role as] citizen or senator or commander-in-chief; for at this point we are investigating the orator. Who is more dignified than he in praising? [Who] more harsh in censuring? [Who] wiser in his opinions? Who more precise in his adducing of proofs? All the virtues of oratory will be found in his highly illustrious orations. Furthermore, what flower or what light of eloquence does his [book entitled] *Origins* not possess?

Why, then, are Lysias and Hyperides loved while Cato is ignored? His diction [*lit.* talk] is too old-fashioned, and certain turns of phrase [*lit.* words] are rather rough. [Yes,] for people spoke that way back then. I know that he, as an orator, is not yet sufficiently polished in style and that something more finished should be sought. [Yes,] for nothing is at the same time both invented and perfected. But it is ignorance on the part of our [orators] that they, the very ones who are delighted by a primitive simplicity in Greek literature, do not even notice this in Cato. They wish to be Hyperideses and Lysiases; I praise them [for that], but why do they not wish to be Catos?

OLD AGE IS NOT A TIME FOR DESPAIR

O most pitiable old man, who does not see that death [in the course] of so long a lifetime ought to be made light of! Either death should be disregarded completely, if it extinguishes the soul, or it should even be wished for, if it leads the soul away to a place where it will be eternal. What, then, do I fear if, after death, I am going to be either not extremely unhappy or else exceedingly happy? But the young man hopes that he will live for a long time; the old man is not able to hope for the same thing. The young man, however, is to foolish to hope [*lit.* hopes foolishly] [for a long life]; for what is more foolish than to prefer uncertain things to certain, false things to true? The old man, who has no [such] hopes, is nevertheless happier than the young man and has fewer cares, since that for which the young man hopes is already his; he [the young man] wishes to live for a long time, [whereas] the old man has lived for a long time.

And yet [*lit.* although], good gods, what is "for a long time" in the nature of a human being? For even if someone has lived for a very long time (there was, as I see recorded, a certain Arganthonius who had lived 120 years), any period in which there is a terminal limit does not seem long to me. Indeed, the hours and the days and the months and the years pass away, and the time, once it has passed, is not ever recalled, nor can the future be known. We ought to be happy and content with the time that is given to us.

Translation of story for Chapter 28:

TWO LOVE POEMS BY CATULLUS

Let us live, my Lesbia, and let us love; and let us value all the rumors of overly critical old men at [the worth of] one penny. Suns are able to set and rise again; when this very brief light [of ours] has set once and for all, we must sleep for an eternal night. Give me a thousand kisses, then a hundred; then another thousand, then a second hundred; then, when we have made many, many kisses, let us throw them into confusion so that we [ourselves] do not know the number of kisses, and so that some spiteful person is not able to find out the number and be jealous.

You propose to me, [O love of] my life, that our pleasing love will be perpetual. Great gods, let Lesbia be saying this honestly and sincerely so that we are able to spend our entire life together in this most happy friendship!

Translation of story for Chapter 29:

QUINTILIAN PRAISES THE ORATORY OF CICERO

Indeed, the Roman orators can make Latin eloquence equal to Greek; for I would match Cicero with any of them [the Greek orators], even Demosthenes. I think that the virtues of these [two] orators are similar: judgment [*lit.* plan], arrangement of ideas, method [*lit.* reason], in short, all the elements that are related to invention. In their oratorical style there is some difference: Demosthenes is more concise, Cicero more elaborate [*lit.* richer]; Demosthenes always fights his battles with cunning, Cicero with authority; in Demosthenes there is a more studied effect [*lit.* more of care], in Cicero a more natural artistry [*lit.* more of nature]. Marcus Tullius, however, seems to me to have expressed the forcefulness of Demosthenes, the copiousness of Plato, the delightfulness of Isocrates. For who is able to instruct more carefully, to move more emphatically? Who ever possessed charm so great that it could sway even the most serious juror? Now in everything that he says there is such great authority that it is shameful to disagree, and he seems to have the credibility [*lit.* trust] not of a legal advocate but of an eye-witness. Not undeservedly, therefore, was Cicero said by men of his own generation to rule in the law courts, and posterity gives to him such great glory that "Cicero" is no longer regarded as the name of a man but of eloquence [itself]. Therefore let us regard this man; let this model be set before us; let a person recognize that he has made progress when he has learned [*lit.* who has learned] to admire Cicero.

Translation of story for Chapter 30:
PLINY WRITES TO HIS FRIENDS

I am angry; I do not know whether I ought to be, but I am angry. You know how unfair love sometimes is, how immoderate it often is, how rather prone to complain it always is. I do not know whether this reason [for my anger] is just; nevertheless it is great [in intensity], and I am deeply upset, because there have been from you, for so long now, no letters. You can appease me in just one way, if now at least you will send [*lit.* will have sent] me very many and very long letters. This alone will seem to me a true way of excusing yourself; all the other [excuses] will seem false. I will not listen to "I was not in the city" or "I was too busy"; and may the gods forbid [*lit.* not allow] that I hear [from you] "too ill." Consider how much concern I have for you. I desire to know what you are doing and what you have done. Now send very many and very long letters! Farewell!

For a long time I have taken into my hands neither a book nor a stylus; for a long time I have not known [*lit.* do not know] what leisure is, what rest is, what, lastly, that idle, yet agreeable [state of] doing nothing, being nothing, is: so many business affairs of my friends permit me neither to withdraw from Rome nor to study literature. For no studies are of such importance that one's duty to friendship should be neglected. Farewell!

Translation of story for Chapter 31:
LUCRETIA: PARAGON OF VIRTUE

Rome was being ruled by a haughty tyrant, whose son was Sextus Tarquinius. On a certain night, when Tarquinius was drinking wine with his friends, each began to praise his own wife. Collatinus said that his Lucretia excelled all the rest: "Let us go to my house and see what my wife is doing now. Then you will know how much more virtuous [*lit.* better] my Lucretia is than the others." They all replied, "Let us depart!" When they had come to that house, they found the faithful Lucretia not playing [idly], but spinning wool. Sextus, when he saw how beautiful and chaste Lucretia was, was overcome by lust [*lit.* an evil love]. A few days later, when Collatinus was away, that man returned. After dinner had been served [*lit.* brought forth], he was led into the guest bedroom. In the middle of the night he came to the sleeping Lucretia: "Be silent!" he said. "I am Sextus Tarquinius; I carry a sword in my hand. Submit to me, or I will kill you!" Although Lucretia preferred to be killed, nevertheless Sextus finally conquered her chastity. Then he departed. But Lucretia told all these things to Collatinus, who swore that he would kill Sextus. Then Lucretia killed herself, lest she seem [*lit.* so that she not seem] to serve as a bad example for other wives: "I free myself from blame, but I do not free myself from punishment," she said, dying.

Translation of story for Chapter 32:
VERGIL PRAISES THE RUSTIC LIFE

O exceedingly lucky farmers, for whom the very rich earth willingly pours forth an easy means of living! Pleasant leisure, fields stretching out far and wide, caves and fresh lakes, and the mooings of cows, and sweet naps under a tree are not [things] absent from them. Among them, rights and laws remain longer; crimes are forbidden. He lives happily who has been able to learn [*lit.* recognize] the causes of things by means of his reason and who has expelled all fears and the worst anxieties from his mind by means of the light of knowledge. Neither do fierce wars frighten him, nor do savage armies, nor do the other dangers that people very often fear. He does not love riches and honors so strongly that he is willing to lose the benefits of rustic life. Although he is poor, nevertheless he seems to himself to be equal to kings when his small children run up to him quickly and offer their dear kisses very freely. To this man the immortal gods, faithfully worshipped, give perpetual peace. Romulus and Remus once lived a similarly blessed life.

Translation of story for Chapter 33:

THE HELVETIANS PARLEY
WITH CAESAR

Caesar undertook war against the Helvetians, who were invading the fields of the neighboring tribes. When in one day he had been able to build a bridge across the Arar River and to lead his army across, the Helvetians, who had accomplished the same [feat] [only] with great difficulty in [the space of] twenty days, sent ambassadors to him. They spoke thus: "If the Roman people make [lit. will make] peace with us, we will remain in the territory where you wish [lit. will have wished] us to remain. But if you have in mind to press us further in war, think about our age-old reputation. For we have learned from our fathers and ancestors in such a way that we wage war more through valor than through treachery. But if you were to lead your army against us, you would surely forfeit [lit. lose] not only your safety but also the honor of the Roman people."

To them Caesar responded thus: "Even if I were able to put aside my memory of your earlier offenses, I certainly would not be able to forgive your recent crimes. Unless you hand over [lit. will hand over] some hostages, I will not make peace with you."

The Helvetians, if they had yielded to Caesar on that occasion [lit. at that time], would have met with a better fate [lit. found a better fortune]. But they arrogantly replied, "This custom has been handed down to us by our ancestors: Helvetians accept hostages, they do not give them."

Translation of story for Chapter 34:

SALLUST'S VIEW OF HUMAN NATURE

All human beings who desire to be superior to the rest of the animals ought to strive with the highest might not to pass through life in silence just like cattle, which nature has made bent forward and obedient to [their] stomach. But all our power has been situated in both mind and body; we use the authority of the mind, the service of the body; the first [trait] is shared by us [lit. common to us] with the gods, the other with the beasts. To me it seems more proper to seek glory with the aid of native intelligence than with the aid of physical strength, and, since the very life that we enjoy is brief, to bring about a memory of ourselves as enduring [*lit.* long] as possible. For the glory of riches and beauty is changeable and fragile; virtue [on the other hand] is considered [to be something] illustrious and eternal.

But many mortals, given over to [their] stomach and to sleep, have spent their lives [*lit.* life] uneducated and uncultured, as if [they were] sojourning in a foreign country; for them in fact, contrary to nature, the body has been a [source of] pleasure, the mind as a burden. I judge the life and death of these people to amount to the same thing [*lit.* to be similar], since nothing is said about either. But, finally, he seems to me to live and to enjoy [his] life who, intent on some pursuit, seeks the fame of a splendid deed or noble profession.

Translation of story for Chapter 35:
A CONVERSATION FROM ROMAN COMEDY

MENEDEMUS: I have one young son. Ah, why did I say "I have"? No, on the contrary, Chremes, I had [a son]; now it is uncertain whether or not I have one. CHREMES: Why? ME: You will know [the story as soon as I tell it to you]. He had begun to be too fond of an impoverished girl. I was always admonishing him: "My son, you should be eager for riches and political offices, not for the deceitful games of love. When I was your age, I found rewards and glory in the army." Now Clinia has gone off into Asia Minor with the soldiers to serve the king and please me. CH: What are you saying? ME: If only I had not persuaded him! I have most gravely injured my son, whom I ought to have helped. I cannot forgive myself. Accordingly, as long as Clinia is suffering many misfortunes on my account, I myself will also pay penalties, working in the fields, being thrifty with my resources, serving him [while he is] away. CH: I think that you are not of a hostile disposition toward your son and that he, indeed, is willing to obey you. But you did not know him, nor did he know you, sufficiently. You never showed him how much you valued him, nor did he dare to trust you. But I hope that he will be [back] safe with you [soon]. Spare yourself, Menedemus! [Your] absent son wishes you to do this. ME: You ought not to be surprised if I prefer to keep working. CH: If you wish [it] so, fare well! ME: And [may] you [fare well]!

Translation of story for Chapter 36:

A CRISIS IN ROMAN EDUCATION

"I think that students become very stupid in schools, because they hear or see nothing of these things that we have in [our daily] experience, but [rather] people, full of fear, begging pirates not to throw them into chains, but [rather] tyrants writing edicts by which they command sons to cut off the heads of their fathers, but [rather] kings warned by oracles to sacrifice three virgins lest a plague become [*lit.* so that a plague not become] more severe. Those who are brought up among these [sorts of set themes] are no more able to be wise than those who live in a kitchen are able to smell good! For with trivial and disgraceful declamations, the teachers have caused the body of oratory to weaken and collapse. Surely neither Plato nor Demonsthenes came near this type of exercise!"

Agamemnon did not allow me to plead further: "I confess that the teachers err in these exercises, but we ought to forgive them. For if they do not say [*lit.* will not have said] what pleases [*lit.* those words that please] the youth, 'they will be left alone in the schools,' as Cicero says. [The ones] worthy of blame are the parents, who do not wish their children to learn under a strict rule. Now, as boys, they play games in the schools; as young men, they are laughed at in the forum."

Translation of story for Chapter 37:

HORACE MEETS A BOORISH FELLOW

I was going along the Sacred Way, as I am accustomed [to do], minding my own business. A certain man, known to me only by name, ran up and, having snatched my hand, said, "How are you doing?" "Fine [*lit.* sweetly]," I said. When he kept following, I, seeking desperately [*lit.* miserably] to get away [from him], was sometimes walking faster, sometimes coming to a halt. He kept on talking, praising the roads and Rome. As I was making no reply to him, he said, "[I can see that] you are terribly eager to leave." "I am going to the house of a certain friend, far across the Tiber," I said. "I have nothing to do, and I am not lazy; I will follow you." We had reached the temple of Vesta, with the fourth part of the day already passed, and he had to respond to a lawsuit; if he were not to do that, he would lose the case. "Please," he said, "stay here so that you may help me!" "May I perish if I know [anything about] the civil laws," I said. "What should I do?" he said. "Should I abandon you or the lawsuit?" "Me." "I will not do it." Then Aristius Fuscus, a friend dear to me, runs up. I grab his hand, nodding, rolling my eyes, so that he may rescue me. "Surely you have something that you wish to speak with me about," I say. "I remember well, but I will speak [with you] at a better time; you will forgive [me]; it is necessary for me to go away." He escapes and leaves me under the knife. Then the opponent in the lawsuit runs up to that man: "You most shameful person, where are you going?" he cries out in a loud voice, and [then he asks me], "May I call you as a witness?" I offer my earlobe for him to touch. He hauls that fellow off into court. Thus Apollo saved me.

Translation of story for Chapter 38:
CICERO SPEAKS ABOUT THE NATURE OF THE SOUL

No origin of souls is able to be discovered on earth. For in souls there is nothing mixed and solid, or anything that seems to have been born and formed out of earth, nothing not even [something] either liquid or airy or fiery. For there is nothing inherent in these elements that has the power of memory, thought, and deliberation, [nothing] that retains the past and anticipates the future and can comprehend the present—which are [abilities] solely divine. Something unique, therefore, and [something] distinct from these customary and familiar elements is the soul's nature and [its] power. Thus, whatever that thing is that perceives, that has intelligence, that lives, that thrives, must necessarily be heavenly and divine and, on account of that, eternal. Nor indeed can divinity [lit. god] itself, insofar as it is grasped by us, be understood in any other way except [as] some sort of unfettered and free intellect, separate from all mortal material, sensing and moving all things, and itself endowed with eternal motion. The human mind is of this sort and of the same nature.

Translation of story for Chapter 39:

CICERO EVALUATES TWO FAMOUS ROMAN ORATORS

Marcus Antonius, as if [he were] a commander stationing his troops, placed all [of his] words in the most advantageous parts of his oration. He used gestures not for the sake of representing words, but for the sake of illuminating thoughts. Although his voice was rather husky-sounding by nature, even this defect was transformed into an asset [*lit.* a good]. For [his voice] had a certain [quality that was] doleful and suitable both for creating trust and for arousing pity. It is necessary, as Demosthenes says, for the orator [who is] desirous of swaying emotions to regard delivery as [the skill] most valuable [to him] in speaking.

Even if I do indeed bestow upon Antonius praise so great as I now have stated, nevertheless in Lucius Crassus there was the highest dignity, [and] coupled with [that] dignity was [his] elegance in [*lit.* of] speaking Latin. For [just] as Antonius had incredible power either for calming or for stirring up emotions, so in interpreting, in defining, in unfolding the spirit of the law no one was better than Crassus. That was recognized in the case of Manius Curius. For at that time Crassus spoke so much [*lit.* many things] against the letter of the law [and] in favor of the spirit of the law that he defeated a very learned man, Quintus Scaevola, with the abundance of his proofs and examples. For this reason Crassus was thought to be the most skilled legal expert [out] of [all] the eloquent [speakers], Scaevola the most eloquent [out] of [all] the legal experts.

Translation of story for Chapter 40:

HANNIBAL AND THE ROMANS FIGHT TO A DRAW

A savage storm was hindering Hannibal's army as it was crossing the Apennine mountain range: a great [shower of] rain, mixed with wind, was battering [*lit.* attacking] the heads of the soldiers, who feared that they could not tolerate such an intense cold [*lit.* so great a force of cold]. For two days they remained in that place, as if besieged. Many men died, many animals [died]: even seven elephants [out] of those that always up until now had survived, perished.

After he had marched down from the Apennines, Hannibal moved his camp to Placentia and, having advanced ten miles [from there], he took up a position. On the following day he leads 12,000 infantrymen, 5,000 cavalrymen against the enemy; nor does the consul Sempronius avoid battle. And on that day there were three miles between the two camps; on the next day they fought with great courage. At first the force of the Romans was so superior that not only did they win but they [even] pursued the routed enemies into [their] camp and attacked the camp. It was already the ninth hour of the day when the Roman general, since there was no hope of capturing the camp, ordered [his] soldiers to withdraw entirely. When Hannibal heard this, having sent out [his] cavalry, he himself immediately broke out from the middle of the camp, [together] with [his] infantry, against the enemy. They fought violently, but night interrupted the battle. 600 infantrymen and 300 cavalrymen from each side fell; but the Romans had the greater loss because so many men of the equestrian rank were killed, as well as five military tribunes and three prefects of the allies.

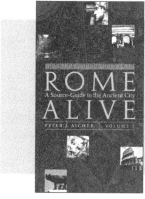
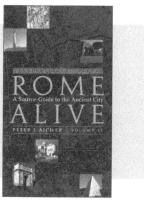

NEW AND RECENT TITLES

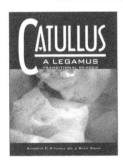

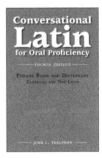

MUSIC HATH CHARMS TO TEACH LATIN

The Mellifluous Approach

CARMINA POPULARIA
(2005) CD, Order Number **00003**

O ABIES (Oh, Christmas Tree)
Christmas Carols in Latin
(2003) CD, Order Number **00001**

VERGIL'S DIDO
MIMUS MAGICUS
Limited Edition CD (1997) 40-page libretto
in Latin, English, and German
ISBN 978-0-86516-**346**-1

SCHOLA CANTANS
(1998)
Cassette: 19 pp., ISBN 978-0-86516-**357**-7
Music Score: 46 pp., ISBN 978-0-86516-**358**-4
Cassette and Music Score Set:
ISBN 978-0-86516-**404**-8

LATINE CANTEMUS
Cantica Popularia Latine Reddita
Illus., vii + 135 pp. (1996)
Paperback, ISBN 978-0-86516-**315**-7

LATIN MUSIC
THROUGH THE AGES
Book: xii + 87 pp. (1991, Reprint 1999)
Paperback, ISBN 978-0-86516-**242**-6
Cassette: ISBN 978-0-86516-**249**-5

CARL ORFF: CARMINA BURANA
Illus., 165 pp. (1937, Enhanced reprint 1996)
Paperback, ISBN 978-0-86516-**268**-6

ROME'S GOLDEN POETS
Limited edition CD, ISBN 978-0-86516-**474**-1

BOLCHAZY-CARDUCCI PUBLISHERS, INC.
www.BOLCHAZY.com